IF POLAR BEARS DISAPPEARED

Lily Williams

WAYLAND
www.waylandbooks.co.uk

THIS IS THE ARCTIC. It's an ecosystem in the far north of our planet. Few animals call this land home. The ones that do live here are

strong,

tough,

slow

and ...

... sometimes hard to see.

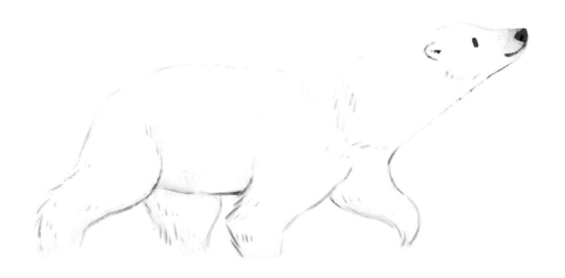

Polar bears are believed to have descended from the common brown bear about 400,000 years ago. As brown bears moved farther and farther north, they evolved to fit their new environments.

Over time, they became perfectly suited to the icy Arctic tundra. They use the sea ice to travel, hunt, and find a mate. Even their white fur is an adaptation to this snowy, treeless landscape.

Although they're the top predators in the frozen north, polar bears are still vulnerable to threats like pollution and habitat loss. But the biggest threat to polar bears and other animals in the Arctic ecosystem is the melting of sea ice because of climate change.

If too much of the sea ice melts ...

... female polar bears wouldn't get enough food to build the layer of fat they need before giving birth to cubs in their dens.

Without enough food, polar bears would be weaker than they should be, and females would have fewer cubs. Some of the cubs wouldn't be healthy enough to survive.

The lack of available food would also cause hungry polar bears to travel outside their natural habitat, forcing them to compete with other predators.

These difficulties would cause the number of polar bears to drop, and before long polar bears could become extinct.

If too much of the sea ice melts ...

... other Arctic wildlife would be affected as well.

If polar bears become extinct, the number of ringed seals, the polar bears' main source of food, could increase at first. However, because ringed seals also rely on sea ice to mate, hunt for fish and rest, they would struggle to adapt to the new landscape, too.

If too much of the sea ice melts ...

... ocean predators like orcas would be able to catch more seals, which would cause seal populations to go down even further. With fewer seals as prey, orcas could move south, disrupting the balance in the predator—prey relationships in those waters.

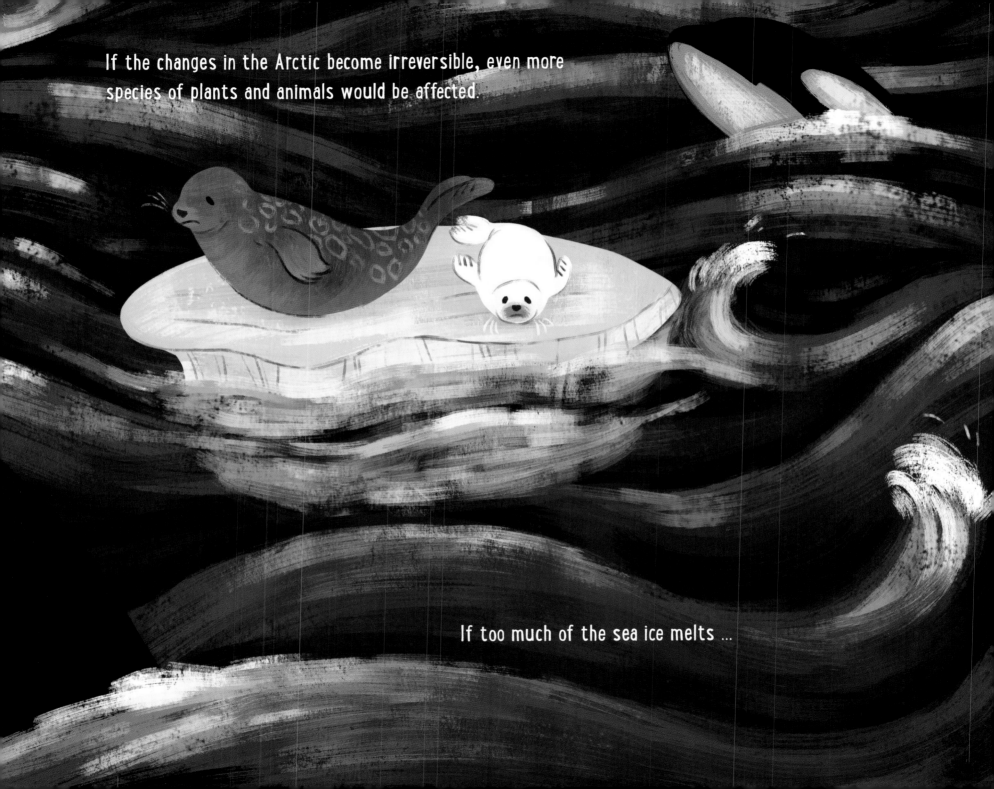

If the changes in the Arctic become irreversible, even more species of plants and animals would be affected.

If too much of the sea ice melts ...

... the Arctic north would grow even warmer and the landscape would change permanently.

Shrubs that were once hidden under snow ...

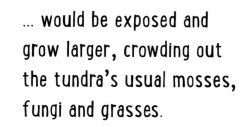

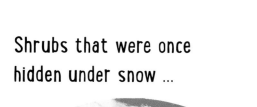

... would be exposed and grow larger, crowding out the tundra's usual mosses, fungi and grasses.

Many of these plant species that are not used to growing in this changing landscape could disappear ...

... causing herbivores like caribou to struggle to find enough food.

Without enough snow, mammals like lemmings, who make their dens in the snow, would lose their homes ...

... exposing them to the harsh weather and predators, and decreasing their populations.

SNOWY OWL

ARCTIC GROUND SQUIRREL

ARCTIC HARE

With many of the small mammals gone, predators, such as the snowy owl and the Arctic fox, would lose their main food sources, just like polar bears did.

Higher temperatures would also alter the mating patterns of insects, which in turn could change the migration and breeding patterns of northern birds, who eat insects.

ARCTIC FOX

ERMINE

WILLOW PTARMIGAN

FRESH SNOW

WIND-PACKED CRUST

DENSE SNOW

ICE LENS

DEPTH HOAR

NORTHERN COLLARED LEMMING

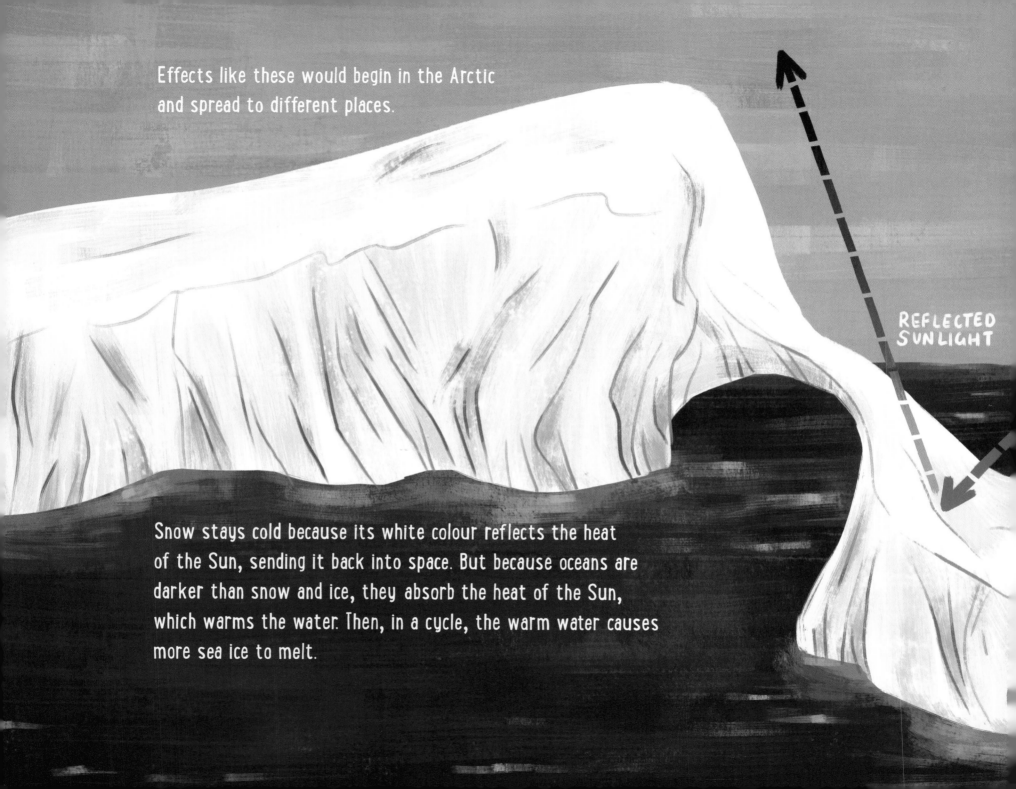

Effects like these would begin in the Arctic
and spread to different places.

REFLECTED
SUNLIGHT

Snow stays cold because its white colour reflects the heat
of the Sun, sending it back into space. But because oceans are
darker than snow and ice, they absorb the heat of the Sun,
which warms the water. Then, in a cycle, the warm water causes
more sea ice to melt.

SUN

SUNLIGHT

SEA ICE
REFLECTS HEAT

WATER
ABSORBS HEAT

ABSORBED
SUNLIGHT

This cycle could continue until all the polar ice has thawed. Then, neighbouring ecosystems could change and their wildlife could disappear. This chain event would roll onwards, affecting all the different ecosystems, from the redwood forests, to the hot deserts, to the frozen Arctic, until ...

... we are no longer able to stop it.

Luckily, we still have time to save polar bears and slow the loss of Arctic ice. Scientists and researchers are working hard to find solutions and educate people about how ecosystems and organisms are connected to one another.

The best way for you to help is to learn everything you can about climate change and how it affects environments like the Arctic. Taking action will lessen its devastating effects.

And maybe we will find that the answer to saving polar bears ...

... has been right in front of us all along.

GLOSSARY

ADAPT: when a living thing changes to help it survive in a new environment.

ANCESTOR: an individual living thing that lived in the past, and from whom other individuals are descended.

ARCTIC: the area of land, sea and ice around the North Pole.

CLIMATE CHANGE: a change in the usual climate and weather of Earth.

DEPTH HOAR: large crystals at the base of a snow pack (also known as sugar snow).

DESCEND: to originate from a common ancestor.

ECOSYSTEM: a system of living and nonliving things interacting in an environment.

ENVIRONMENT: all the living and nonliving things in a place or region.

ERMINE: a stoat in its white winter coat. Stoats are small mammals.

EVOLVE: the way living things gradually change over time.

EXTINCTION: when a species dies out completely.

HABITAT: the place or area where a living thing makes its home.

ICE LENS: a porous, thin layer of ice with cracks that forms as a film atop snow, dirt, or water.

MIGRATION: the movement of birds or other animals from one place to another, according to the seasons.

POLLUTION: contamination by an unwanted or harmful substance or thing.

SEA ICE: frozen water on the surface of the ocean.

TOP PREDATOR: the top predator in a food chain. A predator hunts other animals (prey) for food.

TUNDRA: the flat Arctic regions without trees and where the ground below the surface is always frozen.

THE ARCTIC IS IN TROUBLE

Our world relies on a delicate equilibrium to stay healthy, and man-made climate change is the largest contributor to a growing imbalance. According to the National Oceanic and Atmospheric Administration, fifteen of the sixteen warmest years on record have occurred since 2001. With temperatures rising consistently, the sea ice in the Arctic is melting at an alarming rate. When too much sea ice is lost, sea levels will rise. This could eventually drown some islands, greatly alter coastlines, and severely impact the fragile Arctic ecosystem. If there's inadequate sea ice, top (apex) predators like polar bears could disappear completely, as could marine mammals, such as ringed seals.

If less—or no—snow falls, animals such as lemmings and hares that live and are protected within the subnivean ecosystem will be vulnerable to predators, and their numbers will decline. That, in turn, will affect foxes and wolves, which prey on them. Different kinds of ground vegetation could grow as the soil absorbs the warmth of the Sun. This could decrease the populations of herbivores like caribou. And without sufficiently cold temperatures in the winter, the Arctic mosquito population could increase so much that they could swarm and prevent the remaining birds and mammals from feeding, starving some and driving others away. The Arctic mosquito is relentless in its pursuit of blood, often causing interruptions in the feeding patterns of caribou.

The challenge posed by climate change in the Arctic is unique because, unlike areas of the world where you can replant trees or fence off plots of land, once the temperature stays above a certain level, sea ice won't refreeze. The higher Earth's temperature rises, the worse the effects of climate change will be, and the more likely the Arctic will be changed forever.

HOW YOU CAN HELP SAVE POLAR BEARS

You can help save the Arctic by making environmentally friendly decisions to help reduce climate change:

- Reduce your carbon footprint: walk, cycle or use public transport, and share car journeys when possible.
- Ask an adult to check whether your electricity comes from a renewable energy source.
- Turn off lights and unplug other electrical devices when they aren't being used. Make sure the lightbulbs and appliances you do use are energy-efficient.
- Recycle your waste and purchase products that have less packaging. Look to see if you can participate in your community recycling and composting programmes.
- Ask an adult to turn down the central heating in winter or the air conditioning in summer.
- Eat locally produced, seasonal food where possible. Check out nearby farmers' markets and local producers.
- Eat less meat. Consider eating vegetarian food at least once a week (join meat-free Monday).
- Write to your local MP asking the government to support renewable energy projects.
- Learn about climate change and tell other people about it. Spread the word!

AUTHOR'S NOTE

The information in this book is a simplified description of a complex process. To learn more, start with the Find Out More section on the opposite page.

I believe that when art and science are combined, we can create something powerful that inspires learning. The *If ... Disappeared* books started with sharks in *If Sharks Disappeared*, but now I am travelling the globe to learn about what happens in different ecosystems. Thank you for joining me on my journey!

While some of the information in this book includes educated guesses about what might happen, those guesses are based on the best research available from scientists who have studied the Arctic and the rest of the world for many years. I also consulted with Shelby Angalik, a Nunavut, Canada, resident who kindly spent time teaching me about the Inuit people and the realities of life in the icy north. Shelby is an Inuit, the indigenous people of Alaska, northern Canada, and Greenland. In a lot of places around the world, climate change is considered a problem that will arise in the distant future. However, climate change is already a problem for the Inuit because the warmer temperatures and melting ice affect hunting and travel, disrupting their way of life and threatening their deeply held culture.

Climate change is a pressing issue right now, and we can help slow this process. Start by working together to spread facts like the ones in this book. I hope it inspires you to go on a journey yourself, whether it is in search of the truth within the pages of other books, or into the world on a daring adventure. Let's save polar bears – and the planet!

ACKNOWLEDGMENTS

This book would not have been possible without the following people who assisted me in my research and encouraged my exploration: my family, who always believes in my dreams; Minju Chang of BookStop Literary Agency, whose constant support allows me to leap; Emily Feinberg of Roaring Brook Press, without whom none of this would exist; Roberta Pressel of Macmillan, for taking everything to the next level; Nancy Elgin of Macmillan, for her attention to detail; Alysa McCall of Polar Bears International, who advised me with kindness and the cold, hard facts of Arctic science; and Shelby Angalik of Nunavut, who generously shared a glimpse of her world. To them all, I am deeply indebted.

FIND OUT MORE: BOOKS AND WEBSITES

Go Green! by Liz Gogerly (Franklin Watts, 2018)
Your Planet Needs You!: A kid's guide to going green (Science Museum/Pan Macmillan, 2009)
The Ice Bear by Nicola Davies (Walker Books, 2008)

The World Wide Fund for Nature (WWF) website has a fact sheet on polar bears as well as a resource called 'Ends of the Earth', which helps children learn about the North and South Poles at:
wwf.org.uk/get-involved/schools/resources/ends-of-the-earth

NASA Climate Kids website gives tips on how children can help tackle climate change at:
climatekids.nasa.gov/how-to-help/

Find out all about the work of Polar Bears International on their website:
polarbearsinternational.org